AF477358

HENRY'S JOURNAL

The Historical and Scientific Society
of Manitoba.

TRANSACTION No. 31.—SEASON 1888-8.

HENRY'S JOURNAL,

COVERING

ADVENTURES AND EXPERIENCES

IN THE

FUR TRADE ON THE RED RIVER,

1799--1801.

A PAPER READ BEFORE THE SOCIETY, MAY 4, 1888.

BY

CHARLES N. BELL, F.R.G.S.,

FIRST VICE-PRESIDENT OF THE SOCIETY,

HON. FELLOW ROYAL SCOTTISH GEOGRAPHICAL SOCIETY, HONORARY CORRESPONDING
MEMBER MINNESOTA HISTORICAL SOCIETY, CHICAGO ACADEMY OF SCIENCE.

WINNIPEG:
MANITOBA FREE PRESS PRINT.
1888.

HENRY'S JOURNAL
COVERING ADVENTURES AND EXPERIENCES IN THE FUR TRADE ON THE RED RIVER, 1799-1801.

CHARLES N. BELL

YE GALLEON PRESS
FAIRFIELD, WASHINGTON
1982

ISBN 0-87770-270-5

HENRY'S JOURNAL.

Experiences of a Visit to the Red River in 1800 by Alexander Henry.

An Interesting Paper read by Mr. Bell before the Historical Society.

A meeting of the Historical Society was held Friday ev'g. with the Hon. Gilbert McMicken in the chair. The following paper was read by Mr. C. N. Bell, the 1st Vice-President of the Society:

Deposited in the Library of Parliament at Ottawa is a manuscript entitled "Journal of Alexander Henry to Lake Superior, Red River, Assiniboine, Rocky Mountains, Columbia and the Pacific, 1799 to 1811, to establish the fur trade." The journal is included in two large volumns, covering some 1,600 pages of foolscap, and an introductionary note gives the information that Henry was the nephew of the celebrated Alexander Henry. who travelled through the Indian Territories in 1760 to 1776, and also published his interesting narrative, dedicated to Sir Joseph Banks, the great naturalist.   This note is signed by one Geo. Coventry, who re-wrote the journal from Henry's papers.   He explains that Henry, to amuse himself in this solitary region, first made the memoranda, and later on, the writing afforded him a pleasing recreation, which was continued up to the date of his death. In Harmon's journal will be found an item, dated on October 18th, 1814, concerning the news he had just received of the death, by drowning in the Columbia River, near St. George, of Alexander Henry and D. McTavish, on the 22nd of May, in going out in a boat from Ft. George to a vessel called the Isaac Tod, which lay at anchor without the bar at the mouth of the Columbia.   I have also the original journal of John Macdonald (which has never been published), who left Henry in charge of Ft. George in April before the accident occurred, and who had been the Northwest Company's officer in charge of the Isaac Tod, in so far as the mercantile interests were concerned, on the voyage out from London via Cape Horn.   In this journal I find several references to Henry being at Ft. George, and also a statement regarding his death by drowning.

I have limited this paper to covering Henry's notes from July, 1800, to June, 1801, in the hope of being enabled later on to add more papers on the subject to tne Society's collection.

Alexander Henry, who had been engaged in trading with theSaulteaux from the year 1792, appears to have spent his first season in the Northwest (in 1799-1800) at a winter post of the Northwest Company situated near the foot of Fort Dauphin Mountain, west of Lake Manitoba, leaving there for Grand Portage, the annual gathering place at Lake Superior.   In the latter part of July, 1800, he started on his return to the Red River.   At this time Grand Portage was still the headquarters of the Northwest Co. in the west.   The place was abandoned in 1803, as it was situated south of the Pigeon River, within the bounds of the United States, the new fort being established at the mouth of the Kaministiquia River, with the name of Fort William, being called so after Wm. McGillivray, the chief partner of the Northwest Co.

From Grand Portage there was a portage of nine miles to Ft. Charlotte, the route from there leading through the network of lakes and streams to Rainy river, thence via the Rainy river, Lake of the Woods and Winnipeg river to Lake Winnipeg, where the brigades of boats took their departure for the several districts on the Red river, the Saskatchewan, Athabasca and elsewhere.

Henry, on the Rainy river, found old establishments of the H. B. Co., at the Long Sault and below the entrance of the Rapid river.   At the mouth of the Winnipeg river also the H. B. Co. had a post, near to Fort a la bas de la Riviere of the N. W. Co.   The remains of an old N. W. Co. establishment still existed at the Portage d' Isle on the Winnipeg river.

On the 16th of August Henry arrived at the "Grand Marais" on Lake Winnipeg and found the dead bodies of grasshoppers piled upon the shore to a depth of nine inches.   He describes a stream entering at the south end of the lake under the name of Catfish River.

Passing up the central channel of the Red River delta, which was the one always used by the traders, the River of Death (Nettley Creek) was reached, and soon after, flowing in from the east side, "Riviere Qui de Boule," which rises, like the Catfish, in the Cypress Hills east of the Red River. and near the mouth of this stream was an island.   Describing the "Sault la Biche," (St. Andrews Rapids), Henry writes, "at this spot (at the head of the rapids) where there is a beautiful plain upon the west shore, which is more elevated than that of the east, formerly the Crees and Assiniboines were accustomed to assemble in large camps to wait the arrival of the traders."   Pelicans were num-

erous in the **rapids, while fish in shoals** frequented the spot, the varieties mentioned being sturgeon, catfish, pike, goldeye, &c. Moose, red deer, bears, wolves and foxes also abounded. Truly a sportsman's paradise.

Continuing up the river, "passed Frog Pond, which lays upon the west side (at Kildonan church) and soon after the Riviere la Seine," and arrived at "the Forks," (Red and Assiniboine rivers) on the 18th August, to find forty Saulteau Indians awaiting his arrival, and soon he procured dried buffalo meat in exchange for liquor. Here the trading goods were divided, part being for Portage la Prairie and part for the Red river posts. Five boats of the Hudson's Bay Company's people from Albany river on Hudson's Bay, with Robt. Goodwin, master, in charge, passed up the Assiniboine, and while the transportation of the Hudson's Bay Company's goods was effected by means of birch bark canoes, the Hudson's Bay Company used "boats which carry 45 packages of 80 pounds each, are four-oared, with a steersman, and are neatly built, painted and sharp at both ends."

The men caught plenty of fish with hooks and lines. "Pigeons are also in great numbers here, the trees are every moment covered with them." Henry makes a most interesting statement regarding traces of the early French occupation on the north bank of the Assiniboine. "Upon this spot in the time of the French there was a trading establishment traces of which are still to be seen (where?) their chimneys and cellars stood. I am also informed that there was, at the same time, a chapel and missionary here for several years, but I don't believe they ever made much progress towards civilizing the nations. * * * We are much troubled by swarms of the common water snake. They even come into our tents at midday, and every morning we are sure to find some of them upon our beds. but they are harmless and appear to live and breed in the old graves, of which there is an uncommon number upon this spot, it having been a place of great resort for the nations many years ago. In 1781-2, and at the time the small-pox made such havoc in this country, many hundreds of men, women and children died and were buried here." There is no doubt in my mind but that Henry refers to Fort Rouge, and as he is very definite in stating it was "on this spot" where he was encamped, and as he continually refers to being on the north bank of the Assiniboine, this very clear statement seems to point out that the site of Fort Rouge was north of the Assiniboine, and not south of it. as is the common impression, created by its so appearing on some of the old maps, which were very imperfect as to detail. Even as late as 1870, when 1 arrived at Fort Garry, the thicket of willows and brambles which stretched along what is now the east side of Main street, from near the entrance of

Graham St. south to York St., covered the site of an extensive Indian grave yard, and was evidently the locality mentioned by Henry as the resort of the watersnakes. While in camp at the Forks Henry was visited by a few Indians on horseback who came from towards Portage la Prairie, (the trail was on the north of the Assiniboine). They were "of the tribe called the Snakes, who formerly inhabited the Lake of the Woods. They once were numerous, but at present cannot muster more than fifty men. They may be said to be of the same nation as the Crees, but have a different dialect, something resembling the Saulteau language. They are a mischievous and thieving set of scoundrels, and now inhabit a tract of land upon the Assiniboine river, about 50 leagues west from this place, and indeed some of them are to be found almost all over the country where there is Saulteaux and Crees. I purchased a horse from them for a nine gallon keg mixed rum, and one of my people bought another for the same price. These were the first and only two horses we had belonging to the Red River, the Saulteaux had none, but always used canoes." August 20th, Jno. McDonell, a proprietor of the N. W. Co., with 9 canoes and 3 boats, camped at The Forks en route to Qu'-Appelle, and some boats and canoes of the X. Y. Co. passed up the Assiniboine on the same day.

The Saulteaux with Henry, at the Forks, had left Leech Lake at the headwaters of the Mississippi since 1790. "They were certainly in a great state of alarm when we arrived, and had even made a sort of intrenchment by digging deep holes in the ground, of several yards in length, for the security of their women and children, and for themselves."

During the Northwest rebellion of 1885 the Metis constructed an elaborate system of rifle pits, and it was supposed their leaders had been studying regular modern military tactics, but it is most probable that, from time immemorial, this method of constructing shelter trenches had been practiced by their Indian forefathers.

Leaving the Forks, Henry and his party (which consisted of one clerk, one interpreter, eighteen workingmen, four women and four children) proceeded up the Red River. At the Salle River he notes that the heavy brush, between that stream and the Assiniboine, was a favorite resort of the buffalo during the winter season. On the 22nd Aug., at Crooked Rapids, they found a great plenty of fruit, such as red plums, paubians (pembina berries) and grapes. "The plums are just now ripe and very good. They appear to be of three different sorts—the large yellow speckled, large red and the small red. The Paubian is of a beautiful red, fine and large, but require the frost to bring them to maturity. The same with the grapes, which are of a small sort, and when ripe perfectly blue. Vines are bending to the ground with them." At the entrance of

the Rat River they observed the remains of some old buildings where Chaboiller had wintered 1796-7. A few years prior to this date beaver were in plenty on the upper part of Rat river but were nearly all destroyed. At "Salt Point," above the Rat river, and on the west side of the Red, salt water issued from the bank only a few yards from the river. It is probable that this salt spring is now in the bed of the river, as the annual floods wear away the bank at a rapid rate. Another description of a salt spring is interesting. "Below the Riviere aux Gratia (Scratching river, at Morris,) we passed the great salt pit on the west side of the river. It lays about 100 paces from the water, at the edge of the plain, where it issues out of the ground, forming a small basin, the centre of which appears continually agitated, and to be tumbling up like a pot of boiling water. This, I am told, is an excellent place for making salt at all seasons of the year, as the water never freezes in the middle of the winter, but the process is slow and tedious and requires a large number of kettles to make any quantity, nine gallons of water producing not more than one pint of salt, which is fine and white, almost resembling basket salt having no grain nor coarse substance.'

Vast numbers of Buffalo were seen feeding on the plains about the Scratching River; the willows were beaten down and the bark rubbed from the trees by the animals- The Scratching River, Henry notes, takes its rise in the Hair Hills (Pembina Mountains), under the name of the Riviere aux Islette de Bois, and is divided into three branches before losing itself in a swamp, whence it issues in two streams for 25 miles before coming together.

So plentiful was game along the Red River in this locality that during a morning hunt, while the party paddled up with the canoes, some "few Indians had killed 8 fat cow buffaloes, 3 red deer, and 4 bears near the river bank."

"The Plumb River takes its rise in the Hair Hills in a marsh a little south of the Buffalo Head, from whence running a course passes down the hills and through the level meadows, but in the last place it has no wood upon its banks, excepting at one place where grows a few stunted willows and a chance elm tree. This spot is called the Buffalo's Tent, and is situated halfway between the Hills and the Red River."

Henry is very particular to note every geographical feature of the country, the journal having many items of interest, such as, "a little river runs into the Red on the west side, about a mile below the Rosseau, called the Riviere aux Marais." He says that Rosseau Lake contained plenty of fish, that animals abounded there, and that the French used to go by that route from the Lake of the Woods to the posts on the Assiniboia. His many references to the early French traders proves that information regarding them was then easily procurable in the country. The Indians (Saulteaux) had an alarm at Marais, and Henry writes "I went over to see their trenches. There were three principal ones, about twenty feet long, five feet wide and four feet deep. These were intended for the men to defend themselves in, whilst the women and children would lie close on the bottom. I was surprised to see how expeditious they were, having neither hoes nor spades, they made use of their axes to cut the earth, and both women and children with their hands threw it into kettles, and others into blankets, and toss it up. The Indian women and children lay in the trenches all night, the men in their cabins, (bark tents?)."

Each day a great number of goldeyes, catfish and sturgeon were taken. On the 4th September Henry left Michael Langlois and fifteen persons at the Rosseau river to erect a winter-post; three of the men were afterwards to go to the Hair Hills to trade with the Snakes and Crees. The Saulteaux were dreadfully afraid of the Sioux whose war trail, at that season, extended up to the Hair Hills.

Nine miles above the Marais they camped at the Eagles Nest, and the next day "we came to the Paubian river (Pembina), and crossed over to the old fort which was built (1797-8) by Mr. Chabollier, opposite to the entrance of the river. On the east side of the Red river is the remains of an old fort, built by Mr. Peter Grant some years ago, and was the first establishment ever built on the Red River." The Pembina river is described as taking its rise in the Rib-bone lakes, or Lac du Pla Cotte, and along its course through the prairies its banks "are well lined with large wood, even until its junction with the Red river." Even now there is a fair sprinkling of wood along the Pembina, but evidently in Henry's day the prairie fires had not destroyed so much of it as they have since done. Red deer were very numerous in the woods along the Pembina river, and a short distance above its mouth four otters and three beavers were killed by the party on the bank of the Red.

Pushing on up the Red river, they found the best "salt pit" on the river near the Two rivers, where "the plain comes down to the water and forms an open communication with that of the west side. It is from this circumstance that this spot derives its name of the Bois Perce." Buffaloes and bears were seen at every bend of the river, at one place seven bears were seen to be drinking at the river at the same time.

On the 8th September the party arrived at the Park River, and Henry gives the following particulars: "I went out in search of a proper place to build. I found none so well situated for defence, and wood at hand, as a point of wood on the west side within about a quarter of a mile from the entrance of the little river, a beautiful level plain which divided us

from the river. I should have proposed building at the entrance of the river, but there was no wood on the one side and the land too low on the other." Canoes were unloaded, the lines of the fort marked out and meat stages erected. Game of all kinds abounded, animals resorting to the river to drink close to the camp. The Park River here was quite saline. "The Park River, near which we are settled, derives its name from the circumstance of the Assiniboines having formerly made a park or pound on this river for buffaloes." The water in the river some distance up was good and pure, but a "salt pit" drained into it and contaminated the water.

All hands were soon employed in erecting the buildings, which were made of oak logs and thatched with hay. In one day's time a storehouse was first built. Next in order was the erection of the stockades to enclose the buildings, as fears were entertained that the Sioux would attack them, and Henry writes that, with one or two exceptions his men were cowardly and very much afraid of the Indians, so that "fear was an excellent overseer, and the work went on with expedition." The stockades, which were obtained from a grove 200 yards distant, were of oak logs about twelve feet long. In a week the stockades were up and the gates hung. "We are now in a proper state to defend ourselves and might bid defiance to several hundred Sioux." On Sunday the 21st Sept. "Early this morning the men began to cut down trees to build our dwelling houses. It was their own option to work this day or not, but their excuse is that necessity obliges them to get forward their work as fast as possible, to get under cover before the cold weather commences." It is thus seen that Sunday was respected by the traders in the wilds. Quantities of bear's fat was spoiling because the Indian women were too lazy to melt it. It does not keep unless melted, but when rendered it keeps sweet for a long time. A good deal of mixed liquor was dealt out as gifts to the Indians. The tops of the oak trees in the thickets were broken and torn down by the bears in the vicinity of the fort, the animals being in such great numbers as to cause much surprise to the whole party. When completed the fort had stockaded bastions at the corners about nine feet from the ground.

"On digging a hole, in hopes of finding clay, at eight feet depth we found the carcass of a buffalo which lay about forty feet from the level of the river on a bank covered with oak."

The Indians would cut at the gates with their axes during the night when they wanted to get in for liquor for a "drinking match," as they (the Saulteaux) were not accustomed to having traders erect stockades about their buildings. "It is but of late years that they have seen anything of the kind, and the fellows having been from their infancy accustomed to have full liberty of going in and out of the houses day and night, and being naturally of a haughty, imperious disposition, they cannot bear to be obliged to knock at the gate door that does not open at their demand." Racoons, fishers, and foxes were trapped near the fort. On the 8th October Henry left on a tour of inspection and found a fort had been erected by his men at the mouth of the Rosseau, and a wintering hut at the foot of the Hair Hills. On his return to Park River Fort an Indian presented Henry with "an elegant drum trimmed with all the ceremonies of the Wabano medicine, and a number of different medicines." The Indian expected liquor in return, but Henry would not give any, and remarks, "Gratitude they have none, treat them ever so well and satisfy every demand for a long time, then refuse them but one glass of liquor and all the past obligations are forgotten in an instant, and these persons are your greatest enemies." Henry then set out for a trip up the Red River to Red Lake, and when there was told by an Indian "he knew of no person who had horses in that part of the country." The Saulteau Indians used canoes altogether in travelling. Their summer tents were made of birch bark and were replaced during the winter season by structures made of woven rush mats.

The wolves were very bold and noisy. They did not seem to be hungry and passed by carcasses of animals without eating. "The Canadians swear they are mad wolves, and are very much afraid of them."

Knowing the destructiveness of the prairie field mice, we can easily imagine that they "destroyed dry goods and even carried off glass beads."

November 8th Henry and an Indian started up the Red River to Grand Forks, equipped with a few pairs of shoes, one gallon of high wines and a fathom of tobacco, in case they met Indians. At Grand Forks they saw the traces of a large camp of Sioux who had been there on the war path, and Henry notes that this was a great resort for the Sioux, as there was plenty of game and fish, "and sturgeon winter in the deep water at the junction of the two rivers." Before returning to Park Fort Henry visited the Folle Avoine river and the Otter Tail lake, and writes of the Traverse, Pelican, Cedar and Whitewood lakes, and the "Strong Woods."

At Park Fort, on the 13th Nov., Henry was informed by Indians from Red Lake that J. B. Cadotte was making the Red Lake Portage and would winter there. The men made two kegs of good salt at the "pit" on the Park River.

Hearing that the post at the Hair Hills was in danger from an attack by the Crees and Assiniboines, who were gathering there to send a war party to attack the Sioux, Henry left for the Rosseau and went on to the Hair Hills post (at Pembina Mountain), where he found the war

party had decided to wait for the next spring.

Men arrived with dog trains from Portage la Prairie via Rosseau and the Hair Hills. Mr. Chabollier was in charge at the Portage. One of the men at the fort found a wolf in a trap he had set in a hollow stump, and under it a badger and under that a skunk, all of which he killed, and the Indians at once predicted a great misfortune from this, either to the hunter or to the fort, and were quite certain the Sioux would destroy all the people.

It would appear that the grizzly bear at one time ranged as far east as the Red River, for Henry particularly notes that the grizzly and black bears "take up their winter residence on the banks of the Red River, and generally take to the hollow trees," while those in the Hair Hills resorted to holes in the ground.

"White buffalo are very scarce. They are of inestimable value amongst the nations of the Missouris, but of no consequence at this river, none amongst the Crees and Assiniboines, further than to traffic with the above nations." On Dec. 21st Henry sent a stallion and a mare to Red Lake, to Mr. Cadotte, who forwarded them to Mr. Grant at Rainy Lake, and it is most probable that these were the first horses kept at Rainy Lake. Following the custom of the country at that time, "The Indians are very officious in wishing to provide me a wife, but my inclination does not agree with theirs in the least."

New Year day 1801, was ushered in by the men firing volleys with their guns, which so alarmed the Indians that they rushed to the fort, after secreting their women and children. A liberal allowance or grog was dealt out, and soon every man, woman and child was drunk.

A very interesting description is given of an Indian, who was an oddity. "Berdash, a son of the Surcie, arrived from the Assiniboine, where he had been with a young man to carry tobacco concerning the war. This person is a curious compound between a man and woman. He is a man in every respect as to members and courage, but still he appears to be womanish and dresses as such. His walk and manner in sitting down, his manners and occupation, and language, are that of a woman, and all the persuasions of his father, who is a great chief among the Saulteaux, cannot persuade him to act like a man. About a month ago in a drinking match, he got into a quarrel and had one of his eyes knocked out with a club. He is very quarrelsome when drunk. He is very fleet, and a few years ago was reckoned the most fleet runner amongst all the Saulteaux. An instance of both that and his courage was fully put to the test some years ago, on the banks of the Sheyenne river, when Moneur Reaume attempted to make peace between those two nations. He accompanied a party of Saulteaux to the Sioux camp. They at first appeared reconciled to each other through the intercession of the white people, but on the return of the Saulteaux the Sioux pursued them immediately on their leaving camp. Both parties were on foot, but the Sioux have the name of being extraordinary swift. The Saulteaux very imprudently dispersed themselves in the open plain and several of them were killed, but the party in which Berdash was all escaped without any accident, in the following manner: One of them had a bow which he had got from the Sioux, but only a few arrows; on their first starting, and finding they were pursued, they ran a considerable distance until they perceived the Sioux were gaining fast upon them, when Berdash took the bow and arrows from his comrades and told them to run as fast as possible and not to mind him, as he apprehended no danger. He then stopped and turned about and faced the enemy and began to let fly the arrows at them. This checked their course and they returned the compliment with interest, but he says it was nothing but only long shots, and only a chance arrow could have hurt him, as they had nearly lost their strength when they fell near him. His own stock was soon expended but he lost no time in gathering up those of the enemy that fell near him, thus he had a continued supply. Seeing his friends at some distance ahead and the Sioux moving to surround him, he turned about and ran full speed to join his comrades, and the Sioux after him. Soon after, the latter again approached them very fast, when Berdash again stopped and faced them with his bow and arrows and kept them at bay until his friends got a considerable distance, when he again ran off to join them, and the enemy after him. And thus did he continue to manoeuvre and keep them at bay until they came to a spot of strong wood into which they entered, when the Sioux dare not approach them and returned back to their camp. Some of the Saulteaux who were present at the time, have often recounted the affair to me."

Henry writes of the partiality of the female wolves for the traders' dogs, and that they enticed the dogs out of the fort. In January, Hamel, the man in charge of the Hair Hills post, was plundered of all his goods at the Bulls Head by the Sonnants. "My men having little to do, they therefore amuse themselves by sliding down the bank on sleighs, from the south gate. The descent is so great as to cause their trains to run to the opposite side of river. The Indian women join with them and they have excellent sport." So we find that toboggan slides on the Red river are nothing new.

"Delightful weather for the Indian womon te play their favorite game of coullion upon the ice. They generally keep it up to dark, whilst the men are always employed at their favorite game of platter, and others beating the drum to keep chorus with their wabano songs."

About the end of March sugar-making

was in full operation at Red Lake, where a large quantity of maple sugar was made. "My men are now employed in making soap for themselves with tallow, and when a certain k¹nd of salt is added, it makes excellent soap, hard and dry." Bald eagles were seen all winter and early in March the raccoons began to come out, and buffalo were in plenty. On March 12th geese and swans were seen, and the ice on the river began to break. "The small bastard maple trees ₍begin to run. The sap of this tree makes a fine white sugar, but it is not so sweet as that of the roal maple, and requires a greater amount of sap. There is also to be found, in this part of the Red River, abundance of 'Bois tors,' ⱥ short shrub that winds up the stocks of larger trees. The wood is soft and spongy with a thick bark. The latter is often made use of by the natives as a substitute for provision in the time of famine. There are two species of this shrub; the one grows much thicker than the other and is of a very sweet taste, but of too astringent a nature. The smaller is of a more insipid taste and less pernicious to the constitution. The₎ cut it into pieces and boil it a long time in water, when the bark is peeled off and eaten without any further ceremony. I have often subsisted on this bark, for many days, but always found my weakness increased upon me."

Chabollier and John Cameron arrived with the winter express, for Grand Portage. The express left Athabasca on the 1st January, and, at least on this occasion, went via Red Lake and Rainy River.

Henry states that it was a common disease with their dogs to have a swelling in their necks and die before ten day's time. On the 1st April the river was clear of ice, and for days the carcasses of buffalo, often in whole herds, went floating past. "It really is astonishing what quantities must have perished, as they formed one continued line in the middle of the river for the part of two days and nights. One of my men found an entire herd of buffalo that had fallen through the ice in the Park River, and all drowned. They were still sticking in the ice." Again, after a month's interval he writes: "Buffalo still drifting down stream. It is most intolerable the stench arising from the vast numbers of drowned buffalos that lay along the banks of the river in every direction, above and below, and of which we can see no end. They tell me it passes all imagination the great numbers of buffalo that are lying along the beach, and on the banks above. I am informed that almost every spring it is the same, but not always in such immense numbers as this."

For some reason, not clearly made known, it was decided to abandon the Park River Fort on the 4th May, and very interesting information is afforded us by the following entry in the journal, under date of May 17th. "I went up to the Pau-bian River (from Rosseau) on horse-back, to find a proper spot for building. I got there at twelve o'clock, crossed over the Red river (to the east side) with Desmarais, and planted my potatoes, (30 small potatoes had been obtained at Portage la Prairie) and sowed a few garden seeds on the spot where Mr. Grant's fort stood. We came back, and after examining the ground, we pitched on the north side of the Paubian river on the point of land between that and the Red river, about one hundred paces from each. The ground was so encumbered with fallen trees of very large size, and the underwood so intricate, that we could not see ten yards before us, however, I drew out the the place as soon as possible. Between this spot and the plain on the west are great numbers of fine large oak trees, very proper for building, and on the north side between this and a small rivulet, there are plenty of fine large whitewood proper for flooring and covering, the stockades must be hauled from some distance below where there are fine patches of poplar. This being settled, I remained here for the night and slept in the old fort on the south side." This old fort was inhabited by Charles Chaboillez (written by Henry, Chabollier), in 1797-8, when he was visited by David Thompson, the astronomer of the Northwest Co. The town of Pembina, Dak., now covers the sites of these two forts, and the woods, with the exception of a few trees, have long since disappeared.

"Early on the 18th (May) we returned to the Roseau river and found the Indians were busy employed in making the grand medicine, a ceremony performed every spring, when they all meet, and when there is always some novice to be admitted into the mysteries of that great and solemn affair. On this occasion two young men, a woman and Mons. Langloi's girl were recived. There are many curious circumstances concerning the admittance of women into this great mystery of mysteries." The next day the post at Rosseau was abandoned, and the people embarked for the Paubiau river, where, for the summer, the following appointments were made: M. Lang·lois, principal Indian trader; Desmarais, in charge of the garden, horses, fishing, &c.; Le Diec, conductor of the work: with Rainville, Dubard, Hamel, Poulivette and Le Boeuf, to hunt. Henry then left with his canoes for The Forks, en route to Grand Portage, Lake Superior, to the annual gathering of the Northwest Coy's people. On arriving at The Forks, (now the city of Winnipeg), he made the following entry in his journal: "No news from the Assiniboine River, only that they are starving at Portage la Prairie and exist only on Esquebois, a root about the thickness and length of a man's finger, and may be termed the wild potato of this country. It has a thin skin of a yellowish color, the inside perfectly white, and when boiled is tolerable good eating. They

are also eaten in their raw state but are then of a windy nature, and some times cause a severe colic, which is not easy to relieve. I have known people to suffer very much after eating a moderate quantity. We take plenty of sturgeon, cat fish, lackaishe (gold-eyes), and other kinds peculiar to this river." Two days after he makes an entry which may be considered as closing his journal for that "trade year." He writes, "I set off on horseback for Portage la Prairie, where I arrived at dusk and found all hands actually starving and not a mouthful to eat. 1 remained here until the first of June, when we embarked for the Grand Portage, in a light canoe, with eight men."

Henry's further experiences on the Red and Saskatchewan rivers and the Pacific Coast, of which I possess notes, must form the subject for papers at a future time.

COLOPHON

This evaluation of the journal of Alexander Henry, by Charles N. Bell, was printed in the workshop of Glen Adams, which is located in the sleepy country village of Fairfield, southern Spokane County, in Washington state. The text pages were photographed from the 1888 Winnipeg (original) printing. A fresh title page, colophon page, etc. were set in type by Miss Kristy Frisbie using an Editwriter computer photosetter. Camera-darkroom work was by Evelyn Foote Clausen. The film was stripped, opaqued, and plates made by Robert LaTendresse who also printed the pages on a 770CD Hamada offset press. The paper stock is sixty pound Simpson Opaque, wove finish. The printed sheets were folded and assembled by Evelyn Foote Clausen and Miss Kristy Frisbie. Binding was by Glen Adams. This was a fun project. We had no special difficulty with the work.